Anna Cates

The Darkroom: Poems

The Darkroom: Poems
Anna Cates

Acknowledgements:

Scars Publications 'God Save Us All: Poems with or without the Revolution': "Cinderella Story," "Dreams," "Synchronicity," "Life Psychiatry," "Cain," "Millennium New Year"; Scars Publications 'Gemeinschaft: Poems for the Common Good': "Rendezvous," "Yellow Dogs Run" "After Thanksgiving," "Lobster after Decision," "The Lunatic," "Friend," "The Republic"; Scars Publications 'Paper Cuts: Poems for the Bruised': "Battery Man," "The Flatulence Papers," "Social Theory," "Tarzan," "Strange Mythology," "Training Rhesus Monkeys," "Wonderland," "Snow White's Stepmother," "The Fall," "The House the Beast Built," "The Darkroom," "The Fallen Ones," "The Open Door," "Jesus Jones," "Getaway," "Rituals," "Coney Isle," "Battlefield," "The Civilian," "The Man Who Loves Pain"; The Subway Chronicles: "February 10"; PoetryMagazine.com: "Crows," "Passing through the Fire"; Sorrowland Press 'Dance to Death': "Land of the Broken"; Poetic Monthly Magazine: "Today," "Subliminal in A Minor"; GNU: "Hell," "New World Order"; Underground Voices: "Vegan Cookout"; Dual Coast: "Pedestrian"; Inwood Indiana Press 'Tracks': "Russ"; Codex: "The Second Coming"; Poetry Quarterly: "Honky," "Lament of the Last Haiku," "Odysseus"; Specs: "A Day in April," "Cougar," "Excavation," "Mad Lib: A Poem," "Crickets"; Englyn: "Red Roses"

Finally, I would like to thank Indiana State University for awarding "Coney Isle" the Arion Prize for poetry (Fall 2001); Writer's Hood for honoring "The Darkroom" as "poem of the month" (September 2003); Ohio Poetry Day for awarding "Wheel of Fire" the prize of honorable mention; Conrad Balliet of Conrad's Corner for reading my poetry on WYSO 91.3 radio (Yellow Springs, Ohio).

The Darkroom
©2017 Anna Cates
Cover image: Licensed by Prolific Press Inc.
Published by Prolific Press Inc., Johnstown, PA.
ISBN: 978-1-63275-099-0
Edited by: Glenn Lyvers
Assistant editor: April Zipser
Printed in the USA

"To see clearly is poetry, prophecy and religion all in one."
—John Ruskin

Contents…

Forensic Files

War Songs

Dreams Deferred

FEBRUARY 10

A crime took place on the subway.
What?
The executives look around.
A hand reaches for a briefcase,
And an eyeball quivers at scattered light.

Deadlines crowd in on February 10
As cockroaches crawl on a fallen calendar.

Tonight, the homeless don
Watercolor coats and dollar blankets.
Their tattered map suspends with time.

Snow melts in the dumpster—
Drowning garbage and yesterday's newspapers.

But the doors switch God's children—his very children.
Sunlight lands on 7 brass door knobs.
Night turns cold as glass.

Russ

The most innocent of things
Gave him ideas—
The Good Will painting, gifted by his grandfather,
Of the succulent lady
Slurping up mussels
Sitting upon her bustle
At the seafood bar—
Russell

Referencing him, one townsperson would say
You don't walk your cat like a dog
And another,
But you can't put up a privacy hedge—thieves love that!
While one of the church girls maintained
He only needed to fix his teeth. Then one Saturday
The preacher's wife offered she'd heard
His blue Buick had been parked beside Adult Books
Out on the highway . . .
He caused quite a fuss—
Russ

Police couldn't find anything on him
But everyone knew
In the fustiness of brusque—
Russ

Not queer enough for politically correct
Nor expressly pedophile to warrant an arrest—
Just the Town Pervert no one could trust—
Russ

The villagers came to believe
That when a sly autumn turns to pumpkin orange
A full moon's blush
And leaves rust—
Russ

In the deepening dusk
A lone man heads for trouble—
Russ

Pedestrian

A new year passed. My gay friend with the glass eye
received, just today, his settlement.
And me. A complication thwarting mine,
I've knuckled down to my bereavement.

God have mercy, how his gaze used to rove
each carpool to the vet. Such trees, such calculations
   of sky,
and how a mind and body must yearn so for love.
The crash like a nuclear blast! Not the average guy.

Life isn't fair. Being a fag-hag-Buckeye
from corn-row, I suggested in goodwill a humble renga
   party
during which time, he wrote about it (*the glass eye*)
and made me feel a gracious and forgiving host.

I'm sure it must suck (and I try not to look).
The stiffness in my spine keeps my tongue tied.

Such suffering. Such loss.
"Just a jamb in my printer!"
I laugh it off.

Rendezvous

They ate cheese slivers and crackers for breakfast
After the sun woke them from sleep
Rising like some naughty thing
Around the lake-side cottage
As the open window swallowed up
The musty smell of lust.

They lunched on chicken salad with black coffee
That afternoon beside the rocky beach . . .

But something was eating them both . . .

They talked of Gandhi and Glastnost
As the cunning little motor-boater
Churned up the lake
Like some archetypal dragon
Then supped late,
Split three sandwiches and a bag of apricots.

Then he asked her why she'd given him crabs,
Like she'd intended to
Or should write down the answer on paper
With her "Hand of Love."

She didn't mean to.
It was an accident.
He came with candy and flowers,
Promising money.

Battery Man

Broken homes,
Broken bones,
Broken lovers,
Once brimming with sincerity,
Broken now and bloody.

Some days black and blue eyes spot the town—
Bruised arms, backs, and thighs.
Tears ooze like cactus juice
Through the wounds and pleas,
For neither did her sighs escape you
Nor did the girly neon sign.

Though innocent smiles brighten the lows—
Patched-up children in patched-up clothes—
Their teething gums and teasing tongues
Just seem to froth up indifference, don't they?
Spaghetti or hamburgers, but who cares either way?
After all the re-heated leftovers and TV reruns,
Your mind's a wilted weed,
You're no Sugar Daddy,
And the family's left town,
Looking for a better man.

So now the horizon looms so strangely silent,
For love took its last breath long ago
And lies like a carcass in the desert.
So, let the Angels regret that you were born,
For just like Lucifer,
Hurled from Heaven like a fallen star,
You've lost your place in glory.

Though in the beginning,
God's minstrels sang,
Aspiring in silted grasses
And a seraph concerto chimed their harmonies,
And silver trumpets sounded with triumphant melodies,
And all creation forgot their duties and celebrated
Out of sheer joy
A union between woman and man—
All is broken now.

The Flatulence Papers

The hourglass drips yesterday's fairytale dreams
Into predictable tomorrows as certainly as cracked eggs
Or bloody monkey brains exude their ooze.

Burned-out bodies bob beside the assembly line
Beneath the lights' dank glow—
Confused heads undream tomorrow.

Stubbly armpits leak like pens
In the foreman's white shirt pocket.
A worker slops a mop across the floor.
Someone punches a timecard into its slot,
Leaving a hole . . .
The countdown . . .
Though we speak in the tongues of Angels . . .

Silence is the devil's crumbs.

But the flatulence papers are done,
No longer blank and empty as a ghost town.
The boss piddles around with his numbers and nouns,
Plinking across the keyboard as the computer hums.

Thirsty for epiphany?
Thirsty as Atlantis ready to submerge
In a sadly-romantic apocalypse.

Somebody's fingers fatten and swell—
Drool slides from a mouth in pain—
Slate slashes a hand in an occasional, unavoidable
    accident—
As water drips from a faucet
Like saliva down a chin and onto a soiled T-shirt.

But the job is no farce, promises tomorrow's sustenance,
Comes like black resistance,
Becomes a refuge from poverty's bombs . . .

But have not Love . . .

The workers take their place,
Driven down from the trailer park to the factory
    this night.
The supervisor sits behind the glass window of the
    office.
He pushes a pencil across a desk and talks on the phone.

He keeps a little basket of pens and clippers
And a pillow on his chair to make himself at home.
But he's had to speak to her again—
Not a rapist or a killer, just the manager,
Falsifying data.

Anxiety collects and dispenses like clouds . . .
Somebody's not been spoken for . . .
She's nothing more than yesterday's paperwork.

Yesterday, crumbled up and wrinkly,
Misses the basket and hits the floor.

Honky

The etymology can be a bit tricky
Perhaps the word emerged
From "Yankee" and "honq"
The Wolof word for pink or pale
But one cannot be sure

Up from the south
Past Tin Pan Alley
The 30's
The bread lines
The Great Depression
Fifty years before A.I.D.S.
The jazz man jives
His tonk piano titters
Hot jazz pie
'Till somewhere
Honky-tonk train blues
Just takes over
Somebody croons
And drunk couples
Boogie-woogie

Honey be my honey bee &
Honey bunny boo

Horny bear
Honey buggin'
Honey don't you shake me down!

Honky-tonk gypsy
Honky-tonk caboose
Honky-tonk heaven or
Honky-tonk blues

Hoochie koochie koo—
Hongaarse rapsodie w/
Hoochee Miss Lou

Hoodle addle
Hoodledeedoodeedoodoo!
Hoombahoomba &
Hoop dee doo—
Honest I'm wild about you!

Honkin' fats &
Honky-funk
Homoresque &
Honky-punk

Hooded serpent
Hoof beats &
Hooray for the Yankee dollar!

Honker's dream—
The hooker hangs over
The sill of the high-rise slum
She still boasts all her teeth
And the new perms have yet
To burn her bald
She waits for the blare of
The hoot man's horn
Announcing him a John—
Honorable Mr. So and So
Hot and ready
He voted Hoover—
Hormones & horn of plenty

Night falls over Harlem
Hook line and sinker
Men toast fingers over flaming waste tins—

There's nothing else to roast
As the lamp posts shine like eyes &
The honey wind blows
Honey on the moon—
Hooray hooray its rayrayraining
Hootin' owl blues
As a Model A rolls up the curb
And parks

Honey-drippin' daddy honks his horn
He'll not hurl himself from an office high-rise
This night or slip inside
The houses of Samson
Hot turkey

Honk honk!
Hootin' and tootin'
Horn power
Blasts and again

The hooker slaps back her head
Her eyes reel like separate planets—
Hope and fear
Hope and hostility
Hopeless dream

"Looks like we got another honky!"

Subliminal in A Minor

A storm cloud sogs
August like a cancerous lung—treks south

Over junkyards baked in stench so reek
It eats the sun

From encroaching ivy   leeks   and bric-a-brac
Locusts spread their wings like little vampires

Whizzing south from Lake Erie
And Honky Dory and Donkey DoMe are friends

The bums buck up and stagger
Back down Vine and Maple

Scavenging   scarlet poppies pimple neighbors
Grass—Scrabbling close digging in garbage tins

Empty—an open mailbox wags slack-jawed in the wind
And Honky Dory and Donkey DoMe are friends

Social Theory

Begins something like this:
Only the strongest survive—
Only the smallest
Crust of the upper 1%—

Meaner than the paper-thin sliver of cake
Slanted onto Scarlet O'Hara's china plate.

She pecked one crumb before lamenting,
"Oh, I declare—I just can't eat another bite!"

The rest of us are floating
In a river like a yellow-haired hound.
Cold currents beat against our steady dog paddle
'Till we lose our upstream pace, floundering,
And burble down the flow,
Subsiding, submerging,
Helplessly, hopelessly downing.

Social theory ends something like this:
Water-logged,
We wash onto the bank,
Beneath deadened brambles
At the foot of the loneliest range
To furnish the soil our fertilizing mange.

Tarzan

Don't let them tell you
You're not a man.
Your mother adored you.
But they snipped you off like a rosebud
And gave you to the apes.

Every Darwinist's dream,
You grew with the animals,
Sucked on a monkey breast,
Ate bugs from fur out of sheer love
As you quivered in the cold.

But high society reclaimed you.
Shaggy and infested,
You agonized through the electric shock
Of walking upright after always crawling.
They dressed you in a blue uniform
Like a perfect little automaton
To try the Boy Scout route.
They beat you down like a nail.
They sucked you dry as an Easter egg.
But corrupt authority would not suffice.
At 16, you changed your pledge
And abandoned thoughts of Jesus Christ,
That lord of the apes.

But at the bottom of your dreams,
Cringing at the thought of Hell,
Dodging spells,
You only wanted one thing:
A woman wrapped in an animal skin.

Strange Mythology

We are fools!
We are fools!
The daisies that bloom
The blood of the rose
The broken-skulled sun dripping gold
On the ripples of a pond—
Even the loon's song
Has deceived us
Nature's beauty
Conceals its pain
Like a tattoo over a pox mark

So, we cry out to the rocks
Wanting to die
But science is silent

We feel!
We feel!
Humanity—the sentient!
We stand
On a high-rise
Debating the jump
Then realize the earth
Doesn't huddle on a turtle's back
As the ancients theorized
But scuttles across the galaxy
Like a crab—
But why?
And by what design?

Someday our rocket will go up
And we'll zoom off to Venus or beyond
But for now, we must linger
In all this majesty
Like blood blisters
Trying to heal

Cinderella Story

"As it was in the days of Noah, so it will be at the coming of the
Son of Man. For in the days before the flood, people were eating
and drinking, marrying and giving in marriage . . ." (Mat 24:37)

Cindy watches the excitement on the news.
The world will never be the same:
"All the God-mongers have vanished;
Aliens must have abducted them,"
Caesar explains.
"Now, every good you can buy just by scanning
Your hand or forehead with a moleculator . . ."
Cindy shuts off the TV
And rotates in the love seat
Toward a lit fire place,
Stacks of greenbacks on the mantle,
Withdrawn fresh from the bank that day,
As useless now as three-leaf clovers
Or baskets of rotting fish.
She tosses them in the cinders.
Cindy remembers the 80's,
Chugging across the floors of dance halls—
Then the 90's, the affairs,
Her career in cosmetology,
The prestige that spread like a blood stain.
But, "We're all going to Heaven when we die,"
Cindy rationalized.

Now, with hair bleached blond as cream
And gothic black liner circling her eyes,
She listens to the radio:
"Caesar Christ will soon be appearing
At the Vegas Civics Center!"

Tonight, she'll set out again.
This man could really be him.

After Thanksgiving

Raindrops fall heavier than yesterday's cheeseburgers and
  turkey.
Pellets pound down like harsh words over a trailer-park
  family,
During the aftermath of feasting.

A son pukes in the shower and just leaves it there—
The phone is off the hook,
But all the flowers have been watered.

A daughter stands before the mirror, drowning,
Screaming inside, mouth open wide—
Fat, where a tan should be.

A mother has thrown herself into bed,
Wishing for a time when her face was not so ripe and
  red,
And heavy arms and legs didn't pin her down
To the mattress like she was dead.

Her hand stretches out, the apple released.
She stares outside the dripping window,
Remembering when she forced herself to jog.
The sounds of rain keep speeding up
Like runners that catch up with you, then pass you by.

Yellow Dogs Run

Yellow dogs run down country roads,
Smacking up dust with leathery paws,
Graying their sun-tainted hair.

Yellow dogs run through country fields,
Seeking the weasel's home or poor rabbit's lair
To bury their scent-famished snouts in.

The farmer's wife opens the pantry door
And tosses scraps to the ground:
Curdled yogurt, tuna pie, dried pork chops,
Corpses of poultry and beef—
A small open grave of animal bones
Are devoured amid yelps and burps
'Till the yellow dog snarls,
Grappling for the final bone.
Running away, bloody fur drips between his teeth.

The forest has left its mark on him:
A twig, like a pencil, behind the ear,
Clover between the toes,
And raspberry running down his red-stained mouth.
Nettles and burrs cling to his shaggy blond tail.

I spot one snooping around the back porch:
The unmistakable wag, the agile, lifted leg
Beneath the dogwood's drying bracts.
He grins, rolls over and barks uncomfortably,
He's just inhaled a flea, then . . .
Runs: homeward bound hound.

You don't expect a thing,
Then the alfalfa moves,
And there's a yellow dog!

Reclining along the mashed alfalfa
Like Michelangelo's Adam,
He turns to you and sneers: "Sorry honey, but
I'm running away, maybe from love, maybe my past,
And I won't stop till I find what I'm looking for.
But you sure gave me a run for the money!"
His snout quivers, "Men are dogs."
He snickers and strokes his yellow hair.

Lobster After Decision

Here comes a delicacy
Two chelipeds and a telson
Red buttery lobster
A tasty crustacean
That's quickly vanquished with culmination

Here sits a bachelor
In guilty contemplation
Of his consumption
Of this fine crustacean
That's quickly ravished with mastication

With his bib and his napkin
But without his woman
He's dining alone
In lonely contemplation
He's too late to say, "Let's get to procreation—

Hop down to the chapel all dressed in white
And commit our coition."
A knot's left untied; potential has died,
But it took two to tango in a fateful decision.

The fruit of his loins—a symbol of love
Worth no more than a lobster
That ends in digestion?
Symbol or fruit—who gives a hoot?
He's back with his mother and Mr. Bation.

Geophagy

Mud Cookies Recipe—

Ingredients:
Edible clay
Shortening
Salt
Bullion (optional)

Strain with water
Clumps & rock from dirt
Stir in salt & shortening
Shape into patties to
Dry in the Haitian sun
In Cite Soleil
Trash haven
Two-mile slum
Home to 300,000 people—
Sell to the hungry
To fill their bellies
While nearby piglets
Nose the earth &
Lend their droppings
To the soil—

Mud Cookies

Dreams

I dreamt in my chamber of passionate fire
I dreamt in my chamber of all that conspires
But I have seen the downfall of my ego
Through death and broken years
And I have seen the Everest of my ambition
Erode in streams of tears

I have seen the ever-engrossing hours
Misspend my many dreams
As misguided powers
Diffused the fading gleams
While a sickle ripped through all the flowers

Indeed, untimely are these foes
Indeed, untimely the withering rose

Therefore, I have ceased to dream
As if hope and love have died
And I have ceased to dream
Through my legacy of "whys?"
Though I have dreamt in my chamber
A legacy of lies

Excavation

Oh, how I hoped and prayed
But I've seen death
Move
Slowly up a tree
Dry lower branches
From pine needle green
To orange coarseness
Ripe for garden loppers—
Yes, I've seen death
Strangle sapwood
Limb by limb
Level by level
Another fleeting Babel
Crumbles to dust
So now I must excavate
Cut your roots
Snip one by one
Remove you
From your fixed place
And dump you in *Gehenna*
The rubbish heap—
Yet I cannot blame you
It's my fault
Last fall I injured your roots
Ridding my perfect yard
Of your neighbor
The invasive elm—
Underground
I couldn't tell
Roots from roots!
Ah, forgive a prophet's zeal
It's true
It's my fault
Now just this   empty
Aching   space

Hell

In America,
beyond concern for higher gas prices,
the debate over illegal immigration
and the trouble with violence in the Middle East—
somewhere in America,
as you funnel down beyond the macrocosm
that is America
and enter the microcosm
within America
down
into yet a smaller microcosm
and again another
where you descend further
and keep channeling
down and down
further still
as if you were slipping through a spiral
the childhood slide
even a tornado
you sink down
as if you weren't afraid of Hell
and reach within America that tiny
microcosm that is the individual life
where you'll find two lesbians at a burger joint
meeting for a blind date.

"We're all good Christians here in America."
You hear the standard pickup line and note
them take a booth.

No, you don't look back like Lot's wife
and taste the salt on your own lips—
just the salt on the burgers as you live
vicariously through the empathy
you cannot help but feel for any human being
whether you agree with them or not—

For the truth is, in America
sometimes you wake up not in Kansas.
Sometimes prince and princess never meet.
The white horse never appears.
The slipper just doesn't fit, ashes or not.
A shining knight turns into a toad.
And so, a princess pairs up with
an evil step mom or a wicked witch—
Beauty and the Best.

Her head is full of herb lore,
Wicca potions, and spells.

The other sports an 80's mullet—
within her back pocket, a wallet.

The witch sips her black coffee.
She speaks of the macrocosm:
"They can go eat a Ding Dong!"

The mullet titters.
"Da! They can go eat a Ding Dong!"

A truck driver glances over.
A farmer adjusts his overalls.

"We need to lower our voices,"
the witch whispers.
Her coffee's lost its warmth.
She drinks it just for show,
now finished with her burger.

The mullet sips her milkshake.
Cold sugar granules
crunch sweetly between her teeth.

The witch smirks, lipstick on her coffee cup.
"My ex-husband was the typical male.
He liked Vienna sausages."

The mullet scowls with revulsion
and the truth is
you can't help but share their disgust
as you recall another lesbian
you car-pooled with years before
who cited the same complaint against her father
that "he liked Vienna sausages."

Then you slip down again
beyond the present microcosm
and reach the smallest microcosm within America
that is the Vienna sausage itself—

Carefully flavored
mechanically separated
scraps and fat of beef, poultry, and pork
that crumble apart at the touch of your fork
they're so mushy—
sold for thirty-nine cents a can at the Family Dollar—

And as you posit a single Vienna sausage link
you can't help but also note that sometimes
only lesbians tell the truth
that Vienna sausages really are that gross
and what kind of man would want to eat them
and why would anyone want to eat them?

Then you remember again
that P.E. teacher you car-pooled with
and the story she told
about helping her mother relocate
many years after her father's death
and the kitchen cupboards were still stocked
with old, dusty cans of Vienna sausages
because her mother couldn't
just couldn't part with them
for they reminded her too much of her husband
who just loved Vienna sausages—

Then you descend again
like Alice plunging into Wonderland
though you thought you'd reached the very bottom
yet you fall through another crack
like a child slipping through a mine shaft
and you begin to ponder
what Hell would be like for a lesbian
as you hurl downward like a broken elevator—

And after a long fall through the darkness
you feel the jolted crash throughout your bones
for now, you really have reached the very bottom
and darkness encompasses everything
but finally, you can just barely see
as your eyes grow accustomed
that you are cramped up in a tiny room
smolderingly hot and stuffy

at a table with a gross of men
with warty mouths
and all of you are gobbling up Vienna sausages—
you wolf down the little buggers one after another
sometimes not even chewing because
they're so mushy—

And there's no way out for all the walls enclosing you
are cupboards stocked full of Vienna sausages
and your tiny cell's so blisteringly hot
as if the cupboards were brimstone
and you spear up the next mouthful
holding your little pitch fork with blistered fingers
charred from the cinders
and though your eyes burn and sting
from the smoky embers
you notice that even the sausages are sweating
it's just so intolerably roasting—

The fire just keeps burning—
The air is all used up—
yet, somehow, you just keep dying
and eating that never-ending supply
of Vienna sausages.

Land of the Broken

Spring, 2006,
in the year of our Lord,
Jesus Christ, King of Kings,
a Florida woman is arrested.
Her crime? She laid a stillborn child.
Sirens howl. Police cars
arrive in a Vegas of lights
in America
home of the broken pillar
home of the broken dick
land of tobacco and corn.

Somebody watches from the window
in America
land of the Quaker in makeup—

In America
home of the broken dream
of the miscarried embryo's $10,000 funeral.

In America
grotesque caricatures huddle under steeples
and burble prayers like frogs.

In America
they boast they bred like dogs—
two nothing-but-worms intertwining.
Shine the spotlight.

In America
the rotted corpus remains within.

In America
where an Adam—
all mud and ribs—
had his dick broken by an angry wife.

In America
under God
sometimes a dick gets busted.

In America
an old Quakeress warned,
"If you open your mouth too wide,
you'll never shut it again."
Shine the dental light.

In America
where the victimarchist batters her broken arm
where Walt Whitman sprawled out—naked—
upon the grass
where Jews await the Christ
and scientists the next mutation
where George Washington Carver ground nuts
where lightning struck and shattered a dead tree.

In America
the Holy Roller says F.R.O.G.
stands for "fully reliant on God."
His Harley's bumper sticker bears a cross.
His leather jacket's button reads,
"Jehovah Jireh, My Provider,"
in America
home of seven fattened cows—
hens with tongues.

In America
where the Church landed to escape the Church
where the Church persecuted the Church
where Puritan expelled Quaker
where freedom equals diversity
and diversity equals freedom.

In America
where gay couples begged the Quakers to marry them
and the Quakers replied, "Marriage is between
one man and one women," as if to say,
"No bigamy, please,"
in America
where African equals peanut butter
and Indian equals corn.

In America
a fetus is left
in the toilet at the high school prom
and the preacher says that's
the worst evil in America
and demonic minions blush
in America
home of the broken dick of a father
who doesn't look as good as his son.

In America
the Baptist minister's wife
says she's lost one.
Call the police!

In America
a Quaker wears his collar
loosely like a noose—

In America
home of the Wolarys and the Paynes—

In America
that formed the anti-unification confederacy
for diversity in a fractured society
where a spiked heel sunk into mud
and a Bibled Fonz burnt rubber
where an angry mob charred bras
and the enemy became
monkey, pig, worm—
the ugly mouth has spoken.

In America
home of the broken dream of bathroom patrol
the intolerable weak womb
the empty cowboy hat
the Baptist minister's wife
changes her story to "a large bowel movement."

In America
she leaves the bathroom door wide open.

In America
somebody says, "Amen!
Raise the torch light!"

In America
she'll never be religious right again.
Their mouths remain wide open—
aghast!

In America
land of tobacco and corn—

In America
home of Quakers
gargoyles
frogs.

Lament of the Last Haiku

song of the lost haiku
stillborn as nature
perfect fingers, perfect toes,
ears with tiny hairs
like grass
dead at last

with coal ash
tinting water like coffee in a cup

with skies of fire
over nuclear waste dumps

with gmos
code words of questionable corn
and what-to-do with sewer sludge

piles of
things
things
things
I thought would make me happy
an inheritance for landfills

blind seals lament the last haiku
gagging albatross the plastic oceans
and dead zones
violets the acid rains
nature gripped by the neck
before the beheading

O headless carcass of terrain
of thee I sing!

now I look for honey bees
what flowers that remain
in my song of the lost haiku
my lament of the last haiku
stillborn as nature

A Day in April

on lonely Mongolian range
an ascetic staffs his way toward mountain
like ancient Mises of the Greeks
yet I am home alone braving the music
a treble clef of cloud
unmoored from all horizons—
a mirror and coffee stains—
scents of gasoline waft from the street
and spring sprinkles of rain
dodge the sun—
crickets in the mist click song
a counter intuitive symbol
or just a dog barking two blocks down
my own erratic blogging on to a date site
as all the past rolls into one silver moment
announced with sirens or bells—
i do not say that I am power
(ink pen exploding)
I do not say my anus
is the center of my flower—
a homeric epic—Aristotle corrupting
the youth—and Greek style?
a kingdom, a kingdom for a horse!
why am I here (what evidence)
what shall become of me
(a moon stranger than stars)
and how to answer when a young man
asks are you a cougar:

A shape with lion body and the head of a man,
A gaze blank and pitiless as the sun . . .
moving its slow thighs . . .

when we decipher
magnetic vibrations from snake mounds
vibrato musings of the universe exploding
characters from the color purple
or just an eccentric neighbor
(a grandma needing Depends)
we'll find something significant
in the taste of an orange
emanations from the stillness—
original sin—the frog of primeval garden dew

Training Rhesus Monkeys

My friend Jenny says she's found a job
Experimenting on rhesus monkeys.
I see them walk, holding a handrail,
Tails dragging like limp fish flippers.

Monkeys balance their awkward bodies,
Retarded ballerinas, offering gibberish
In the forget-me-not days
Since science interrupted their jungle lives
Amid the vines and tropical plush.

He takes his first step like a human baby.
A scientist sits, quietly pondering,
Another takes feverish notes.
Fingers click across a laptop pc.

Some would say love cannot be measured
In the microscopic lives of amoebas.
No, that's alright.
I know you're not so hard-hearted
As to enjoy animal testing.
You just have somebody else to pity.

Starry, Starry Nights

The House the Beast Built

The madwoman's locked in the cathedral
But she's no longer tied to the bed
But protrudes like a gargoyle at the window
And wishes that she were dead

Crocodiles swirl in the channels
Like the voices invading her mind
The steeple has severed and toppled
But the farmer's fed his swine

Demons dance in the attic
As the fever flickers like fire
Consuming her sleep and soul
And tearing her heart like a briar

The marriage bed is barren
Its posts stick up like horns
The sheets are torn and twisted
Her dreams dried up like corn

She lives and breathes so brokenly
In this house the Beast has built
But she cannot be reborn
Only subside and wilt

Cougar

Proud in thick thighs and lace
I flaunt my ace
Toothpick clean
Young guy's dream

I've rolled a bloke
With hands big as a lobsterman
I've sizzled fat bologna
In a silver fry pan

I'm not the next bitch
I breathe like a witch
The midnight air as
Stars, aghast, buckle and stare

Mad Lib: A Poem
(fill in the blank)

God/the devil _____ (verb)

with a(n) _____ (noun) of_____ (noun)—

the _____ (adjective) _____ (noun)

of a(n) _____(noun)

_____ (verb ending in "ing") us

before _____ (noun)

_____ (verb) _____ (adjective)—

a _____ (noun)

_____ (adjective) _____ (noun, plural)

and _____ (adjective) _____ (noun, plural) of _____ (noun)

only _____ (noun, plural)—

our (adjective) _____ (noun, plural) _____ (adjective)

_____ (verb) out the _____ (noun)

Odysseus
(& His Sweaty Pig Men)

Sirens sing.
Poseidon roars.
Lightning splits the sky
And sea. Coral reefs crush oars
As floor boards destroy
Themselves on the rocks—
Deep at sea,
Odysseus warned
His sweaty pig men:
Medusa's tentacles squeeze.
But thinking rolls back
With mermaid mirages
On waves of loneliness and despair
Like lost ships
Tossed about on blackest seas—
A lighthouse shines on,
Cyclopean eye in the gothic night.
Salt tears seed the dunes
As survivors crawl
Like wet rats to shore.

Wonderland

The mad woman thinks she's queen.
She tears her heart out by the roots.
He listens to her cry
Till his torso turns to paper,
And his head loosens at the shoulders.
He renders his assessment:
"Take pills."

People shuffle in and out.
He gnaws his pencil like a carrot
And listens to each confession:
I was poisoned at a party.
I choked on the shard of a tea cup.
I crawled through the wrong door.
My insides are bloody.
My lungs are full to the nubs.
I remember lying on a mushroom,
Horrified of a pipe-smoking worm.
At five they tweedled me by the sea.
My body dripped sand like an hour glass.

"But how does that make you feel?
And what proof do you have?
Where has the time gone?"

I long for home.
My sister comforts me with words.
Her stories soothe my sickness like chicken soup.

She enters his office unexpectedly.
He's pumping someone up and down.
"You're early." He hops off.
"Where has the time gone?"

He grins like a naughty cat:
"If you pull a tree up from the ground in winter,
You can't tell the roots from the branches.
Still, Alice, if you hadn't slipped, if you'd only held on,
You wouldn't be here right now, would you?
Come on, Alice (*who won't take her pills like a good girl*),
Forget about the past,
Eat me!
Drink me!"

The Fall

Ever tire of questioning?
Ever sicken of sorrow,
Slinking around your neck like a spaghetti noose?
Ever desire the golden eggs of truth?
I do!

One night I hung my head outside and cried.
My tears fell into the soil like colored beans.
A chord bloomed outside my bedroom window.
The braided ivy stretched from ground to sky.
So the possibility was there, I knew.
But I didn't climb it
Till it sprouted leaves and branches.
Then I thought I'd climb that vine!
Why not die?

So I glided up to the Giant—
To the One who squeezes out love for us all—
Who rolls comfort to us
Like a moth ball.

"So can I play the old shell game?
Can I open the carton a little early?
Can I stay?"

A door opens in answer,
And the air takes me.

Now I'm falling.

Now, who's to say

I'm not still

Falling?

Today

Today is not September, 1992
I am not attempting suicide today
And yet I do recall the time I thought
The soiled stink was worth aching about
Purple exploded in kaleidoscopes of color
Rapidly expiring to the dust
Beyond that, it's never purple anymore

Yes, just crazy
Until I cracked
I couldn't think
I couldn't own my face

Yes, just crazy
Until I shattered like glass
My life too lazy to move
My hands too dead to clap
My head a fallen bee, muted to buzz

For a moment, the world became too flat
The daisy dropped to the ground, withered, and died

But today is not September, 1992
I am not attempting suicide today
And so I won't anoint the sleeping pills with oil
And spoon a cake-bowl full into my famished mouth
And wash away the drugstore
With a bottle of cheap wine
Which leaps beyond, of course, just eating my broccoli

Yes, I'm eating all my broccoli!
I'm saying my little prayers!

I am not attempting suicide today!
Not today
Not ever again
I'm painting the sky bright purple

October 22, 2007

The Lunatic

They spot him again outside the convent,
Like a fearless Mt. Everest climber,
Ascending the statue,
Groping his way up the Virgin Mary,
Holding her stone-gray limbs,
And passionately kissing her marble lips.
"Let's run away together,"
He groans, nibbling her pebble lobes.
No answer.

He returned the following night with something to entice her.
He waited for his chance then approached her,
Pulled himself up the pedestal, blushed,
Then popped the question:
"What do you say we run away together?
I need someone horribly,
And I've always loved purity.
Look: Pearls!"
He held his hand forward.
The tiny moons sparkled in the starlight.
No answer.

"You're so hard, Mary; so cold."
No answer.

Weeks later, just when Mother Superior
Thought she'd seen the last of him,
She glanced out the window to behold
Two knobby hands caressing Mary's spine.
"That is enough," she huffed,
Pounding down her fist like a raw onion.
She mustered the troops outside, encircling the statue.
Two nuns with brooms struck him.
He nearly toppled over.

But Mary, stiff as stone, stood her ground,
And despite his pleas, provided, as always,
No answer.

Life Psychiatry

Streets between fences
Weed-filled grasses between tree stumps
Rotting walls of houses between failing gardens
Indians between oceans and memories of pioneers
Even neighbor between neighbor
But just between you and I
And the places time fenced in
Let's remember how love punctured fear
Like a nettle leaving holes
In days like pieces
Like tears
Before we grow old
We sometimes cut ourselves

Synchronicity

Madness prickles like a cactus.
Nature's junior flowers pop up like pun.
But spring won't amend the angry cymbals
Clanging through your head
Or the subtle hands of clocks
Swerving through sadness or time.

Motions and emotions
Swirl like wind-filled crops or oceans.
Cathedrals denounce your friends
And family with dongs.

So you dash off abruptly like a rabbit
For the walls are crumbling
And the rivers invading,
Spilling—so suave—over their sides,
Dumping croaking frogs.

Your frenzied laughter chimes like clue.
Danger looms in circles and angles.

Oh, such bittersweet synchronicity!
Hickory dickory dock!
You stop,
Yes, you stop!

Nude Descending a Staircase

Reminds me of our fractured society
The shattered mirror that brings bad luck
Distorted images in the mind
Pieces of a puzzle that never quite fit

It reminds me of that quote from Derrida
I could never understand
The body of the nude
Reminds me of that Quaker sermon
Mournful about our fractured society
Broken pieces
Like scattered photos
Little vignettes of life
The nude descending
Like lemmings into the sea
Legions, legions!
Yet I'm stultified
Why?

Oh Marcel
You've aroused the Taliban
Legs move like ballerinas twirling
In a painting by Degas
Confusion between Ichthus and Dagon
The illusive fish god
Worship of flies upon dung
And children sacrificed to the fire

It reminds me of Eve numb
Like Snow White
Left holding the poisoned apple

The serpent come
Thy will be done

It reminds me of the cosmos
Exploding into pieces
The voices
In my
Head

The Voices

Van Gogh cut off an ear
He could not endure the voices
Though beyond closed doors
Voices always clatter

Today a rat winks at me
From behind the cactus
And bells chime

Now I have made myself blind
Now I have murdered my mind
Now my palm is an erasure

But the rats linger
Belligerent bells clamor
So angry and cold

The Fear

The fear is like finding yourself
Driving alone in a beat up pick up
Along a deserted road just after dusk.
You wonder where you are going,
Where you have been,
As you glance down and notice the gas tank empty.

The engine gulps then expires.
You exit the truck, slamming the door shut,
And enter a nearby field of brush,
Burrs collecting along your Levis,
Crickets crazier than Van Gogh
Throughout the air as you pass by.
Their skinny legs whizz away from your vortex.

You stop, realizing you're trespassing
On someone else's private property,
Shadowy trees doomed to silence.

You hear the snarl behind you.
Your chest turns to lead.
You turn your head toward a black hybrid
Of attack dog and attack dog,
Goose bumps electric bee stings all, all over you.

His saliva foams like white water rapids,
The growling rumbling deeper than midnight
From within his pith as if no amount
Of mutilation could remedy your offense.

Crucifixion and Dog Food

Brown hills—
Brown sky—
Empty roads lead
From nothing to nowhere—
The cattle cars rattle by

Horse heads
Hang from windows
Tongues loll in thirst
They pant like dogs
Tongues dangle like tolling
Bells, stick like glue

Concave hills—
Sacrilegious sky—
Miles upon miles
The cattle cars rattle by

Ridden concave-backed
Retired whipped-and-spurred
Broken bodies offered
After crucifixion
For dog food

Brown hills—
Brown sky—
Panting for verdant pastures
I too feel a little dry

The Horses of Arabia

Ever wonder
how the horses

of Arabia buffet
the dessert gales?

Neigh, I'd die—
Just thinking of it,

I feel
a little dry.

Scarlet Skies

Once I walked beside the purple lilacs
And Kwanzan flowering cherry trees
Into the woods
Under the shadows beside the bog
Among the pussy willows and cattails,
The brook burbling with crawdads
Then icing over in winter like fairies' lace.

I trod the woodland path,
Checking toadstools for gnomes,
My mind a Kaleidoscope of dreams—
Plastic toys that meant so much,
Ponies crayoned green,
Life still magic.

Now the swing wags empty with the wind,
The garden full of weeds.
The house fades away into the countryside
With secrets to keep—
There is a kind of death
That makes the angels weep.

I used to have a nightmare
Of falling through the dark,
Terrified of hitting bottom,
Terrified too of wolves and bears,
Creeping through the window
From the blackness outside.

The dream ended.
Night turned blood,
A scarring of stars and wind,
Scratching out the sign,
Foul as a goat's hoof.

What a mess of merds!
Nothing but scarlet skies!
First a field of daisies then a garbage heap—
There is a kind of death
That makes the angels weep.

The View from Up Here

"I say climb the mountain." — Dean Young

It began in the slime,
A riptide whirlpool of causality,
A tadpole swimming into frog parts—
A sperm, brainless and eager,
Its bloated head an empty Jack-o'-lantern, molding up inside.

I move on,
Don my backpack and trudge toward the mountain,
Climb high, pickax chipping into ice,
Thinking I've risen above the whole world beneath me.

Yet always I remain under the foot,
The dusty boot that crunches cockroaches,
The dirty thumb of pretense,
Like Icarus beneath his flea-bitten wings, racing the sun,
Or the bomber beneath the metal ceiling of intent just before
the blasts.

I march on like the Mexican,
Hunched beneath his hobo bag in silhouette like Quasimodo,
Jumping the Sierra Madre Mountains for the California factory farm,
To roost for a space with the tortured chickens,
Twisted and compressed into one beast by wire mesh,
In air feathered thick with dander and dung.

Beneath my backpack,
Laden with the all junk to save my life,
I climb the peak,
Build my Babel,
Erect towers in the endless night,
The view from up here, all starry skies,
Not a soul in sight.

From Where I Stand

in the moonlight
clouds move in patterns
like swirling dragons
those cunning devils who know it all
stars poise themselves
like an alphabet of charms
I turn a page
and like a monk
realizing he's been poisoned
I feel the burning fever
of a sick mind
and though I try to pretend all is well
I can't hold back the coughing
my whole neck a gargle of mucous and pain
the tickle exploding
out my nose and ears in a big bang

each star becomes the eye of a gargoyle
glaring down at me
and I wonder
why am I here
alone in the dark
at night on a hill
like monumental rock
solemn as gravestone
naked in the wind
before a haunted forest
glinting with starry eyes of its own
sleet stinging my goose-pimpled skin
as I hold open this book
written in runes I can't even read

Wheel of Fire

Wheel of fire fills the sky—a doleful blue
Where swarm bird multitudes
Always on the move to get away from it all

Wheels whorl
Planets spin
The solar system churns its buttery Milky Way

The universe a hollow donut
Ever-expanding post-bang into what must be
Leaving only dark interlude

The oblivion left behind
An emptiness of emptiness
A vestigial void never filled

A wheel-shaped hole where once was
A nothingness doing nothing
Not even feeling its own absence

Without remorse
A pathos of incomprehension
An irony never understood

There's a wheel within a wheel
And it's burning in me
What then will become of me?

Where

where highway
succumbs to country miles
twilight hints at birds

where paved road
returns to gravel
ginkos thump to earth

where earth and rock
fade to grass
wind forgets itself

where grass
gives way to wilderness
sovereign power of oak

where woods
hide in mountain shadow
gold medallion wanes in the sky

where clouds
circle a nebulous moon
swaying elm dream-catch

The Village That Never Was

Midnight through the window
In the village that never was
A hoot owl darts into dark skies
Toward tomorrow

Morning at the Babel never built
Silence pours into every ear
Till all are buried in the sand—

Windstorms alone disclose the holy grain

Evening after the hour glass expires
The earth tilts in its radial sphere
Always going, going, going
Never taking us

Anywhere

Crickets

in an un-mowed field   e   .
              cri c k   t s .   .

       rain
    the   bow's
at   edge—c r i c k e t s . . .

as dusk
tramples
down
summer
heat . . .

   crickets . . .
with a new moon
serenading earth rhythms—
   crickets . . .

beyond a first date's
midnight kiss:
   crickets . . .

abstract lunacy—
starry, starry nights of
   cricketscricketscrickets . . .

Snow White's Stepmother
(A Mad Woman's Lullaby)

The vacant hill—
The shallow air—
The shadow we call home
That lies on the lawn
Like a paperweight—
Here I'll raise you
I'll teach you to walk
I'll guide your feet
Across the sunless grass—
Each yellow blade compressed
Nothing will escape you—
A distant vessel
A flaming cross
A black-burnt heart—
Sinister breed
Bad baby
Mother of God
I wanted to silence you
To diffuse the acid
Loosed from your mouth
That devours me like hungry fish
Dear God
I gaze at the maze of stars
Outside our bedroom window
And am lost in the calligraphy!
Sinister breed—
Beautiful!
Beautiful!
I'll eat my own poisoned apple
I'll offer my heart on a dish
I'll dangle the moon before your eyes
Then fold you in a blanket
My paper doll
My skeletal white

The Final Chapter

Aaron's rod
the psychic silver chord
of astral projection
a dream drifting
through the fog of night

or loosed from its caboose
as monks meditate upon the dong
and drone their OM
or a head is struck to stone
or a child ripped
untimely from the womb
unraveling into stars
verbascum thapsus
verbatim mantra

once the silver cord loosens
and the golden bowl breaks
once the pitcher ruptures by the fountain
and the wheel shatters at the cistern
mourners stride the streets
funeral torches
from tallow dipped
woolly mullein blaze
in the darkness of night

the owl's eyes gleam
in the darkness of night

the lone dam screams
in the darkness of night

blind fires rage
in the oblivion of night

Forensic Files

The Darkroom

Somebody leaves the darkroom
On Orange-Black October—
A worm wiggles over a corpse,
And a doctor fingers through a birth canal,
Melting the secret icicles of his pregnant nude.

Un-camouflaged scandals
Are exposed in the darkroom—
Lamps radiate with fuzzy blue light,
And photos are hung up to dry.

Her shoulders seemed pinned down,
Touched by the new moon—
He tenses at the bluish-white caesarian scar,
Moves beyond the point,
But stops short of the mark.

She arrived at the military base early
As if to a dinner party—
Now the doctor's uncontrolled hands writhe
Over his naked patient
Like a gothic organist,
Pounding cobwebbed keys.

Street lights glow like the eyes of night
Beyond the covered windows of the darkroom—
A watery envelopment,
A fresh side-shot,
And a camera-ready end,
Then the silent soldier slushes out
But cannot win.

Pregnancy's veteran:
Malpractice hasn't stolen your heart.

Pregnancy's veteran:
Hush!
This isn't Christmas Eve.

The Fallen Ones

Dream's end—
Dead end streets—
Car engines rumble like thunder,
And women hobble by in high heeled stilts
As laughter rolls through broken or golden teeth,
And lust clutches somebody's fallen lover.
But why ask, "Why are you walking the streets?"
Or, "Don't you believe in the eyes of Heaven?"
Painted women will always read their poetry.
Listen to what they say:

Let us help you reach the grave.
You will spill like autumn leaves
And melt like morning dew.
You won't just go into hiding—
You will plunge like a star in the solemn rain
Within a great and towering sky.
You will discover death
As the old folks do,
Dropping to the floor with a rasp—
You will discover death
As the unfaithful lovers do,
Crashing to the bed in a blast—
You will discover death
As the mountain goats do,
Descending the rocky crags beside the monastery,
Trampling down pastures laden with excrement
And cremation's ash,
Sprinkled by priests when the air is still and the sun
Setting behind another funeral procession.
They raise their goatees,
Pausing in morbid fascination,
Realizing they've been eating it!

The Open Door

In summer farmers hoe turnips and radishes.
Blackberries fatten then decay.
But she finds the bush limbs bare
When she parts the icy tentacles,
Bordering the forest.

Beware when the wolf becomes friendly
And moose cross the brink with foaming mouths
And demons ascend the stair.

The farm house has ceilings with holes.
In the cellar, red eyes glow.
A woman curls into a ball
And demons creep up the wall.

Demons can rise from the stink.
Demons can look you through.
Demons can eat an orange whole.

Reality sinks in like a thousand needles,
Twisting muscle.
The baby's cheeks are red with blood.
Her fingers stiffen with the chill.
Mother holds the bundle to her breast
And follows the shadows across the snow.
And a demon hunches his back like a boulder
And bolts through the open door.

Pink blankets in a crib mold in the cellar,
Far away from sight.
And demons with dripping mouths
Linger in the chill.

Jesus Jones

I read a tale of Chinese brothers.
One held his breath for hours.
One turned his neck into a column of steel.
One swallowed the sea to escape the pain . . .

Jesus Jones, clairvoyant,
Presses his nose against the screen.
He can hear it through the walls.
He sputters and fizzes, his face reddens,
And today's Tom Sawyer screams:
"You always tell me things I already know!"
Jesus never stomped upstairs.
Jesus never wanted a crown.
Jesus never threw himself upon his sword.
He knew that girls were raped
And never refused to heal.
Just touching his robe stopped the issue of blood.
Jesus always took his turn.
He walked on the water and didn't sink.

But pain invades a sheltered world.
Every night there's another bone.
The toilet water turns pink.
Reams of torn wallpaper hang in the air.

When Jesus walked the Earth,
Did he share the mind of God?
Did he know that the Star Trek posters
Would be rent from the wall?
Did he know when it would start?
Did he know that she would touch
The blanket to her face
When someone broke her little pin cushion heart?
Did he know that the eyes would collect

Themselves in single file
Along the crack of the closet door—
That the bones would compose themselves
In skeletal form?

Jesus Jones, fully human,
Sits on the pew,
Collar buttoned at the Adam's apple,
Shoes pressed together at the heal.
The speaker knows his thoughts.
He reads it in the bones.
He sings a funny tune.
Prayer spurts from his mouth.
But though he packs his ears with wax
And sits on his hands for hours,
Pain invades a sheltered world,
Bolts fly through the air like bullets,
And the skeletons cross their skinny thighs,
Wishing for the break.

Blood covers everything.
He's sinking in it.
It passes his chin,
And he drowns.

Getaway

At the coast
He spied her,
Casting bread into water,
So content without a grind—
He felt his hope subside
Down to the green sea
Like a gull with a bullet
In its side.

He found her so inviting—
French braid
Thick as rope
Nestling across her back
Like a garden snake—
Pure as beach glass
Slipping grapes between her lips
Alone,
As if she'd found paradise.

He followed her home.
Now,
Hours later,
She's nipped in the bud.
Her lipstick
Shines like a cherry.
She sleeps like a dove.
A tea kettle sings sweetly.
Blood seeps
Into the sofa
Afghan
As he swings
Down the fire escape,
Crafty as a dragon.

Outside, a cloud blots the blue
Far,
Far above him.

Too,
Too bad
His Angel wouldn't love him.

Cain

The fall began as an afterthought.
"Maybe I should taste this bitter fruit—
Pluck at the forbidden vine"—
The thought began in Eve's mind
Then grew into binary plan
Like bubonic plague that can't help but spread
As she shared the surprisingly delicious fruit with Adam,
And she and he tossed away God's will
Like an apple core or a melon rind.

No drizzle had dampened that garden.
Nothing could extinguish love.
Afterwards, they walked away
In scrappy animal skins like dogs.

Cain's path seemed even darker:
"Who'll defend me from these strange new people?"
He must have thought.
"I'm cursed by everyone I meet.
When I walk by, they scowl and stop their chatter.
I'm dangerous, they say.
They won't let me through the town's barrier,
So I must keep traveling,
Hoping to prove myself harmless,
Even advantageous . . .
Surely, if I had God's boon,
For God is fair."
Hearing his bitter pleas,
And noting other men's bloody ideas,
God granted him mercy—
Gave him a mark like a four leaf clover,
Saying, "Here's for a little luck, Cain.
You're going to need it after murder."

Cain saw the fullness of the moon
And journeyed on,
Waiting for the sunrise.

Crows

I

I trudge across the sludgy snow.
February's cold lingers like a mirage among the branches.
Snow clings like love to crofts of trees
And crumbles and falls, like an occasional eagle or sparrow chick,
To the white and green-needle bed
Below the lower skirts of trees.

My rainbow perspective startles me—
Another raw glance at half-frozen and thawing dreamscape,
Spreading open before me—
Evergreens and naked birch bark trees.

I trudge forward in my lesbian boots
As sun meets snow,
Melting the sweet clumps with its ardor.
Waters drown from twinkling ice, and, oh my heart—
Furs exude their twigs and waddle-sticks,
Dispensing them throughout the ditch-pond.

I stake my claim to nature—I drive my spike into a tree!
I know civilization remains undaunted.

Minutes ahead, a highway intrudes,
Meandering through the Rocky Mountains.
Distant Mack-trucks growl like plotting men or plodding dinosaurs
Across the roadways.

I part the branches—
Out on the road, a lumberjack in a flannel shirt
Places a spare tire on his beat-up pick-up.
With his black and white thinking and rapist potential,
He expresses more self-disgust than hatred or fear.
I cock my rifle and aim at the beer belly.

Back at the camp, I won't be unexpected.
Back at the lodge, they won't suspect a thing.
Back at the grill, they'll probably laugh
At my willingness to catch a cold.

A few feet before me, crows peck the ground.
A bitter breakfast of seeds preserves their ailing health—

We all share a common end.

II

I stare at the snow clumps,
Twinkling along the birch.
I find another half-frozen rainbow,
Laughing like a girl across the wilderness.
Ice still clings to furs,
Despite the constant dripping.

The sun warms the black backs of crows,
Confidently finished feeding.
They roost atop the sodden spruce.

I pass the ditch-pond and try to forget
My asphalt encounter.

If a chipmunk had bounded across the road for nuts,
That red-neck would have loved to pulverize it—
If a blue bird had flown low,
He would have grinned to hasten it
To a wind-shield-splattering death.

As the Indians say, we return to the ground
As the snow that melts in streams
And sinks to her foundation of springs.

Though nature consoles an aching heart,
And love subdues baser desire,
Hot water screams from a geyser!

III

All but the toughest clumps of hard-packed snow
Have finally finished melting,
But drizzle suppresses the sun.

The lodge remains on end.
Sickness and soggy supplies
Keep the campers groggy.

Indeed, I must seem innocent.
Indeed, the crows have flown.

I stride through the evergreen
Like thoughts that begin from nothing.

Friend

Once more the weather turns
Frost specks the valley
Trees trade their green
For orange and gold
Crisped leaves descend
Down to the eager pond
Down to its dark glass
Down through its desperate depths
Down to where the catfisherman's soul rests

Winter lumbers forth
A hunter rasps
Fumbling through the brambles
Limbs scratch his orange jacket
Snow drifts
To shadowed branches in wisps
Thickening his steps
Cold drizzle soaks onto his neck
Like a wet kiss

His journey ends
Where the forest fails before a clearing
There moose hover like gargoyles
Over the reflective murk
Where a paddle still protrudes
Like a shark fin
He's lost a "friend"

Vegan Cook Out

Summer looms in a haze over country roads,
sunken between cornfields.
The atmosphere bloats with humidity,
clouds retaining water like an old aunt.
Muskmelons quicken to ripe,
and begonias bloom,
pink and purple faces begging Heaven.

I lean back in the lawn chair,
shaded by a maple,
and suck the fizz off an icy Bud
as the Boca Burgers lose their frozen grimace
on the grill, shrinking from paralyzed to juicy.

One cloud inverts,
extinguishing the sun
and the highlights in your mink brown hair
as you hold the spatula like a scepter over hot coals,
flaunting your culinary skill,
poodle panting at your ankles,
pillars of the temple for his god.

My pen explodes
in the middle of a poem,
soiling my hand with black ink,
and you laugh at sheepish me,
tossing a crunched-up napkin,
looking earthy as a gypsy in your hemp T
and Birkenstocks
as you swat Boca Burgers onto organic buns,
warming tomato slices.

And little do you know,
my sweet and unsuspecting vegetarian,
that hiding behind my poetic facade
is a sty of obscene thoughts,
filthy as a factory hog farm,
ideas crammed together
and biting at each other's tails.

Squealing inside, I swig down the last swill
of tepid back wash and grin,
thinking how tonight
a pig in dress socks
will smear his swine flu all over you
and smother you with his meat.

The Bike

The bike sailed east around Vashon Island.
Spokes sputtered gravel into the fog.
He pedaled on,
Seeking salamanders, cicadas, frogs.

The wheels stopped beside a hemlock.
He chained the bike,
Ducking back into dusky woods,
Seeking salamanders, cicadas, frogs.

Did he lose himself in the wilds?
Get kidnapped?
Join a pack of sasquatch?
Fairies never tell.

Years hence,
Amid the salamanders, cicadas, frogs,
Moss like hillbilly beards,
They found the rusted bike
Grown into a tree
The lost boy fading deeper
And deeper into mystery.

Ferguson

Daylight fades.
The doctor completes his autopsy.
The mortician pulls down the shades.
The sun shuts its lid over a burning eye ball
And a penetrating film of darkness spreads.

It's a new age
Of drones and frozen embryos,
iPads and rampage—
When humanity means everything to itself.

Businessmen hurry home
As prostitutes thicken on the streets.
Poverty clings to cement walls—
Graffiti evolved from crayon scrawls.
Death curls into a ball
And falls down a sewage drain.
No amount of pepper spray
Will wash the drugs and disease away.
Police hound criminals,
Sirens wail,
But here we remain,
And only scared for a minute,
Proceed with a devilish plan.
Proceed . . . deadpan.

Rituals

The sky lifts its skirt.
The moon drops his arms.
The stars are in charades.
The grass rustles.

"There will be blood for drink tonight
And bones for the vultures tomorrow,"
Bael chuckles.

Yellow eyes surround the campfire,
And Pan plays his pipes in the background.

How kind of him to bring her
Into the womb of nature.
It's not so cold.
The stars warm her like light bulbs,
And he is gentle,
Or that's what the crickets say
When the moonlight dims,
And the frost sets in,
And the wind bristles.

The Republic

The lollypop tastes delicious in Kindergarten,
But the God-full hot-gospeler appears unconcerned
At forced intimacy between angel-voiced choir boys
And dry-mouthed seducer-voyeurs.
Parched tongues stick when the curtains drop.

The queer tree-planter grows diseased and finicky,
And the deacon finds him unworthy.

Reservedly contrary,
Demon-warrior zealots battle the evil spirits away
But often never think to say,
"That was you back there behind the elemental curtains
Of everything and everywhere."

So yank back the Republic
Before the idiot-savant-spiritualists.
Let fortune-telling psychics grow sober
And spell-casting witches even more enraged.

Gypsy shamans will chant the day's magic
As city marshals poke their empty vessels,
And love poets pen-worthily write it all down.

War Songs

Riding with Death

in Basquiat's Riding with Death
the bones foretell
a toxic demise
a broom like arm sweeps across gray skies
closing the curtains
to skeletal eyes
we ride our own bones—
a broken-backed horse—
into our graves
warring with ourselves
we die a thousand times
only to mount again the same old bones—
arise to the confinement of our days—
advance toward more gray skies
stick figures
riding
     riding
         riding . . .

Coney Isle

Strawberry delicious lipstick meshes with your desire.
Almonds and cream coat your marinated jowls.
Honeymooners and doves appear off Coney Isle,
Where rule-the-roost pirates once capsized
Sea-sloppy sailors and sycophants.

Did corsets and veils mean to protect the damsels
From the ruin of such octopi?
Tearing apart underskirts,
Those blood-stained wolves plundered and ravished
With a Moorish aye-aye
As whips lashed and revolvers flashed
In the fustiness of brusque—
As elegant as ammonia,
Those ruffians pillaged pilots
And left women as soft as fresh-baked bread
As desolate as hydras!

But today a marine just whistles,
Glancing at the damsel,
Who seems so lonely there.

He patrols his sickened brain like a wizard,
Admiring the diesel lances upon the guard.
He scrutinizes Woodwind Elms in fury at the enemy
Past sections of coast with aluminum valves
But within the icy limber—electric cocoons
And the rush of running water through hydraulic canals.
Now the glorious orders of his superior
Juxtapose subtle falsification in subliminal sanctuary
Like algorithms tackling air were a disembodied head to fall,
Mocking the white gloves
That look like something borrowed from his sister!

Somewhere else,
Along a cobblestoned street, a tour begins.
Somewhere else,
A scholar studies Algonquin.
Somewhere else,
A janitor scrubs a bathroom urinal.
Somewhere else,
A soldier's feeling virginal.

Passing Through the Fire

The Nazis used tools
They mastered fire

Yes, we've all heard
Yes, we all know
They stacked up corpses like corkwood
For the incinerators

But the holocaust began with healthy, normal,
Intellectual skepticism
They denied the sacred scriptures

They craved the old ways
Of the Phoenicians—
A name that simply means "red-head" in Egyptian
Hair flaming as fire
The same people as the Old Testament Philistines
Goliath and Delilah
Who some maintained were of the Aryans
Adamites
Who lived 1,000 years
Before the fall and flood
The "Arya" of the ancient Sanksrit Vedas—
A name that simply means "lords of the soil"
And in Latin "arare," "to plow"
Farmers who tilled the ground
By the sweat of their brow
Though the earth choked up with weeds

The Nazis adopted the primordial symbol
Of the Hindus, the Britons, the Phoenicians
The sacred emblem
The swastika—
That simply meant "sun" or "fire"

Long before it became the ugly spider
Its broken arms turned right

The Nazis revived the primordial mythology
They practiced the ancient sun worship
They honored the Egyptian Amen Ra
They honored Baal
Like the Philistines
At summer solstice
They lit the bon fires
Circled the blaze
Then jumped right through

But they were careful with themselves
Passing through the fire
For having leapt through the flames before
They knew that fire really burns

They smoldered bodies, books
Synagogues, living children

They accepted death through Adam
With all the skepticism in the world

They craved the inferno
They mastered fire

New World Order

"Even the devil disguises himself as an angel of light."
2 Corinthians 11:14

Maybe as children they weren't afraid of the dark
Somewhere in it, a fire always burned
That never extinguished sight
Around it the old Nazis gathered

Maybe they began in brightness then entered shadow
The New World Order promised change
And some girls liked to stroke their prickly heads
They, too, enjoyed it

Maybe they came to believe
It's not so bad to ask, "What would Hitler do?"
To follow him for what he did
And yet deny he did it

Maybe after all the hippies, preppies, and goths
Neo Nazi seemed like just the next turn in the road
They formed a secret society
That, yet, was not so secret

But what fellowship is there with light and darkness?
They cannot form allied forces
Fire cannot dance on water

How strange that even today
All roads lead away from Berlin
The hub of a spiral
The swirling swastika
That ancient symbol of the sun

From there the devil set down his little hoof—
Placed it forward, then the other, and again
Like Dorothy in her ruby slippers
Skipping along the yellow brick road

Maybe he seemed innocent enough
Pigtails and horns—
He smiled that broken-toothed grin
His sooty knees knocked together
Bashfully, like a gay

The Civilian

Mold covers her bread.
She chokes when she swallows.
The deserter takes it
As God's punishment for the war.

He gives her a gift that shouldn't long endure.
But she is gone for hours, and her mother worries.
Yet better than a Nazi, aye?

He shows her scars like shark bites.
He shows her gold-plated lighters that really burn.
He shows her snap shots of fiancés and red-lipped
Italian whores with teeth as straight as cartridges.
He shows her the American way.

Outside the sun sets over charred backdrop.
Mines explode.
Bullets pierce lungs and crack bones,
Tanks roll over rubble with nozzles erect
As middle fingers raised defiantly to God.

The Man Who Loves Pain

There's a man who loves pain.
His only flash of joy
Is destruction.
He strips the earth of trees
And pumps disease into the air.
He'll pluck out a baby's lullaby
Then splinter someone's bones
To show him must how sharp
He really is.

Imagine:
The man who loves pain gets his way—
Hot at the task,
A bead of sweat drops from his brow
Like a nuclear bomb.
If the world was ever a temple,
It's ruins now.

Imagine:
All is finished—
Everything beautiful is gone.
Only the man who loves pain remains.
He sits on a tree stump
With no one to hate or rape
And weeps.

Millennium New Year

Soldiers and prostitutes
Mix in brothel art
Outside the blood-stained fields
Sodden with tears
The fate of these years

Soldiers gurgle and howl
Spill to the ground
Abandoning life
In passion or fear
Now passes the year

Soldiers skirt the next hill
Beyond the dark caves
A tattered flag waves
A drone whisks over shoreline
Where vines meet the blue borderline

Regret haunts the mountains
Of what could have been
Chiseled with waters
The river-ribbon glints and juts
As the ancient sea sparkles

Battlefield

Blue icicles hang
From the tunnel's dark mouth.
From the other end,
Gray bodies wiggle out.

Corpses—some nude—
Some with worms—
Clutter the battlefield.

The cameraman's fingers
Twitch with the cold.
He clicks the next snap shot.
Then dark sky marches out.

Three Little Pigs

America is full of outdated infrastructure
Crumbling highways and electrical grids
Old, debilitated homes
Lopsided and sunken roofs
Asbestos walls
Prefabricated modulars not built to code
Drain pipes feeding sewer gasses into attics
Dryer ducts dumping moisture and lint where they should not go
Bad grades drawing rain water to foundations.

America is full of money desperate people who don't give a damn,
Who can't complain for fear of losing a job.
They'll lob you in the dog house
Before you've time to sing, "What's Going On?"

It's almost as bad for the rich man.
The poor man only dreams of owning a home.
He passes dog houses on his walk to a dead-end job,
    dreaming.
But the rich man knows the little guy lives in shit.
He drives by outhouses every day on the way
Home from work to his mansion beyond the palms.
His eyes are red and weepy from images of decay,
His senses infected with mildew from lean-tos
That can't help but turn his head.

Some people ruin perfectly good homes,
Convert rentals into grow houses,
Basements full of marijuana and mold—
Meth labs and crack houses about their business.

We dropped bombs on Bagdad, destroying homes.
Destitute women stood by the rubble, cursing us to Heaven.
America, the wolf is at the door.
Is it planting a tree or dropping a bomb?
So desperate for money yet in debt
To only finance more wars abroad, wars that never end,
Friends who too soon become enemies
And attack us with our own, gifted arms?

"Little pig, little pig, let me come in!"
What will you tell him?
What have you to say?
Have you built your house out of brick?

American Healthcare

I try and try
To wring water from a dry sponge
But like a bankrupt blood bank
It comes to nothing.

Someday I'll die,
Hiding up in my tree,
My tree house built of my own brittle bones,
A broken coo coo bird of a brain,
A window where a hip replacement should have been,
Another: glaucoma eyes, squinting at splintered plywood,
A trap door: my filth reeking beneath me.

My tree has spent its leaves.
My squirrel has lost its nuts.
Autumn has devastated me.
I shiver into death
Beneath my female-pattern baldness.

Maybe at ninety
I'll be a blob in a nursing home bed,
An entity less significant that the period
At the end of this sentence.

Or maybe not . . .

Maybe at ninety
I'll swivel on my wheels,
Wily as R2D2 beneath a steel gray perm
Like a mushroom cloud,
Smoothing a severed rabbit's foot for luck . . .

Maybe at ninety
I'll be a bionic woman,
Feeling luscious in my Dolly Pardon wig,
Sprinting down the sidewalk
Faster than slow motion
Before the communal town houses,
Absorbing all of life,
My roots thirstier than a willow tree,
All of me
A last generation.

History

wars erase memories
pioneer stories long found in a people
whereas the coal-black ground remains
a stranger takes back the sky and names
so who can bring them rest?

ghosts
still haunt the corn fields
and the scarecrows seldom grin

so have you drifted back
to tired reversions
to times of crowns then crows
with laughter from only a few?

we scour attics
old newspapers and microfiche
searching for answers
finding here and there a clue

Red Roses

red roses
born of spring rain
there's no silver lining
on a mushroom cloud

The Nutrition of the Hippies

At times, you lived off nothing:
Glasses of ice water
Mixed with coffee creamer and sugar packets—
Almost a milkshake.
And free ketchup packets too!

You lucked out with gifted meals
The vitamin A, C, and E of LSD—
Cocaine, heroin, bennies—
Sperm in vertigo—
You didn't have a love child that year

While John Kerry strung testicles with wires
To electrocute the Viet Com
And bombs blasted Saigon
You ate the cracked monkey brains of veterans
Finding a little protein for the mustard & relish packets
Thieved from the next restaurant

You tasted the exhaust of the pick ups
That wouldn't pick you up
On your hitchhike from Berkeley to Washington—
Peace & protest—
Flashbacks in tie-dyed—
Groovy—
Now, so bad and so old

You hated your daddy's money
His fat ass sat on all those dollars and food
His swollen wallet caused him scoliosis

Your best friend, Judas, from Jesus Christ Superstar—
You thought he was your friend—
He wore a white suit too

You abandoned education—
Tuned in, turned on, dropped out
You braved the pigs and the cactus

America saw your point and the excess
And you saw theirs
You stood before each other, naked lovers
Moving to embrace

You nuzzled hairy armpits
And each Mamma Cass
You nested in billowy afros
With no other pillow

But finally, you forgave yourself and God
Realized life is work or death
Got yourself a job
And accepted that paycheck
Like a rat dropping on your tongue

The legacy you left—
Your love children—
Flipped the coin of extremism
As the pendulum swings
They turned up their collars
Izod alligators tickled their nipples
They became exclusive

But you were last seen in Alabama
Some grown up love child
Driving through from San Francisco saw you—
Long beard with the Willie Nelson braids
Mangy tangles beneath the sun-burnt baldness—
He thought, *Aha! There's a redneck kook
If I ever saw one. Free tickets to the zoo!*

O Say, Osama, Can You See?

First you knelt toward Mecca.
Then you titled further west.
Your eyes strain at the sin.
Your mind festers over America
With our B.C./A.D. and our A.C.D.C.
The western star grows dim.
Our gays don't wear a burka.

You watch America.
You watch the West.
Like an Indian sun-gazer
Your eyes grow weak
Staring at all the sin—
At Lucifer descending like a falling star—
Not so bright anymore.

But I've seen the Internet advertisement
For Afghani water-front property
Along with the disclaimer:
"This lake is full of sexually-abused
Camels & goats."

And so, I have to ask you,
Osama, can you see?

Do you discern the blood-speckled banners
As machine guns blast
And mines explode
And poppies wave like grain
As opiates addict young minds
Brainwashed by propaganda?

Dirty burkas trail along behind you in the dust,
And I've a mind to ask you, Osama,

Do you prefer first class or coach?

Yes, Osama, I sin!
I believe in God,
But I'm not God.
I cannot string him along like a puppet.
I cannot tie him down like Gulliver.

No, Osama,
Our gays don't wear a burka.
They laugh at the sun.
They run naked through the rain.
Their toes tease the grass.
They hurl themselves upon each other's back,
Thrusting
Like one camel on another.

Yes, Osama, they sin.
Yes, Osama,
We all drink from the same lake—
Globalism.

So let's just destroy the excess,
Burn all the oil and the grain,
Suffocate our unfaithful lovers—
If we can't have them, no one can . . .

Osama, you stared westward
Till you went snake-eyed.
You watched the camels—
The burkas—
The rain—

And I imagine you did,
From time to time,
Gaze at a goat with lustful eyes.

Ancient Alien

"Wherever the corpse is, there the vultures will gather."
Matthew 24:28

Dow reports—
democracy in $100 plates
& women earning their bodies

new boots—
the credit card's max
& the cost of education & bombs

aid from the West—
sandbag style sack after sack
of unbleached white flour

pin up girls—
doggie style
& feminism

commercialscommercialscommercials—
birds that just keep
clacking . . .

today's capitalism:
an Aztec Jesus lifts
his golden grail—
a toast to you and me—
the ancient alien
boards his battleship
and blasts off into space

the plumed serpent
still bites his dust

the common rabble

still eat

his heart

The Second Coming

Political smut overcasts the sky
the dust bowl
rushing across the plains
while the white pines
whip with the wind—
a pathetic fallacy.
Lobbyists hustle Washington,
full of passionate intensity,
tiptoeing into negative capability,
the futility quivering.
The world's a troll that's turned to stone.
The poem's a lie,
a Disco Word Orgy
that moons the sky
now kingdom come.
Read me! Read me!
it cries. Stanzas
stack up pig pile
like skyscrapers
then tumble
down to dust.
Deserts fill with dragons. Witches
ride their little brooms
like Halloween in July. Oceans wail.
Tectonic plates shift. Planets
line up like skid row inmates for lunch.
The sun shies away with wounded pride,
and the gay men green cheese grin.
Crows grow old beneath their feather boas,
waiting for the beast.

Turning, turning,
the world keeps turning,
waiting for the beast,
hunched on his haunches like Pan—
hairy, breasted, phallused—
Hecate.

Published by:
Prolific Press Inc.
Johnstown, PA (USA)